All about materials

Does it stay warm?

All about heat insulators and conductors

Angela Royston

W

FRANKLIN WATTS
LONDON•SYDNEY

First published in 2009
by Franklin Watts

Copyright © Franklin Watts 2009

Franklin Watts
338 Euston Road
London NW1 3BH

Franklin Watts Australia
Level 17/207 Kent Street
Sydney, NSW 2000

Series editor: Sarah Peutrill
Art director: Jonathan Hair
Design: Elaine Wilkinson
Photographs: Paul Bricknell (unless otherwise credited)

The author and publisher would like to thank Sara Cinamon for her advice
with the experiments.

Picture credits: Alamy: 9t (Matthieu Spohn/PhotoAlto). Courtesy of Blizzard
Protection Systems Ltd (www.blizzardsurvival.com): 29. Construction
Photography: 20t (Chris Henderson), 21b (David Burrows). istockphoto: 12b
(Roberto A Sanchez). NASA: 28b. Shutterstock: 4t (Chryacat), 4b (In-Finity),
5c (Luc), 8 (Elaine Davis), 12t (Anne Kitzman), 14b (Losevsky Pavel), 16
(Daniel Hebert), 17t (Sure C), 20b (Thomas Barrat), 22 (Tomasz Trojanowski),
23t (Germany Feng), 26t (Berto Paeli), 26b (photoBeard), 27b (Denis
Dryashkin), 27t (Paul Paladin), 28t (Dennis Sabo). SPL: 17b (Gusto Images).
Wishlist images: 13.
Cover images: Shutterstock: tl (Dennis Sabo), tm (Elaine Davis), tr
(photoBeard), b (Berto Paeli). Every attempt has been made to clear
copyright. Should there be any inadvertent omission please apply to the
publisher for rectification.

With thanks to our models: Megan Collier, Lily Cornelius,
Jody Humphries, Connor Rose

Dewey number: 530.4

ISBN: 978 0 7496 8723 6

Printed in China

Franklin Watts is a division of Hachette Children's Books,
an Hachette UK company.

www.hachette.co.uk

Please note: The investigations in this book have been thoroughly checked
and tested. We regret that the Author and Publisher cannot be held
responsible for any accidents or injury incurred while following them.

Contents

The topics highlighted above are investigations you can try.

Words in bold are in the glossary on page 30.

Passing heat on

Heat travels from warmer things to colder things. An ice cube melts in warm tea because heat passes from the tea into the ice. Some materials pass on heat more quickly than other materials. Those that pass on heat quickly are called **conductors**. **Insulators** are materials that hold in heat and pass it on very slowly.

Oven gloves are good insulators. They stop heat from the baking tray burning the cook's hands.

Cups

Cups are made of different materials. China cups are hot to hold, because they are made of a material that is a good conductor. Some take-away cups are cool to touch, because the material they are made of is a good insulator. A good insulator will keep the drink hot for longer.

The coffee in this mug is steaming hot. The mug and spoon are also hot, because heat from the coffee has passed into them.

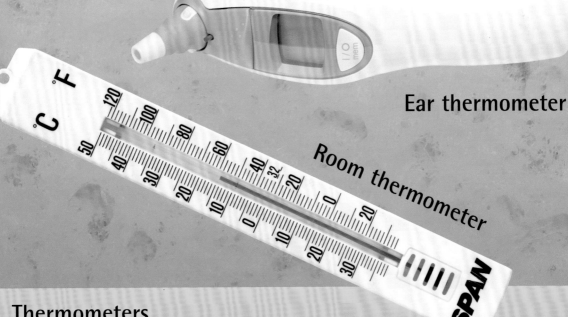

School thermometer

Body thermometer

Meat thermometer

Ear thermometer

Room thermometer

Thermometers

A **thermometer** measures how hot something is. Different types of thermometer are used to measure the **temperature** of different things. A meat thermometer measures the temperature of meat cooking in an oven. An ear thermometer measures the temperature of your body. A room thermometer measures the temperature of a room.

Measuring temperature

You will need:

A thermometer, a glass of warm (not boiling) water, a glass of cold water, ice cubes, paper and a pencil.

This investigation uses a thermometer to measure the temperature of different things. You need a thermometer that can measure from about 0° Celsius to 80° Celsius. School thermometers do this and so do some oven thermometers.

Place the thermometer in the glass of warm water. Wait for the thermometer to reach a steady reading. Write down the temperature of the water.

Do you think the temperature of your hand is warmer or cooler than the water? Grasp the end of the thermometer carefully but firmly. Write down the temperature of your hand.

1

2

Measure the temperature of the cold water. Add several ice cubes to the water and wait a few minutes. Now measure the temperature of the icy water and write both temperatures down.

Draw a large picture of the thermometer on the sheet of paper. Mark the temperatures 0° and 100° Celsius on it. Divide the space in between into ten equal spaces to give 10°C, 20°C, and so on. Add the temperatures you have measured and label them.

3

4

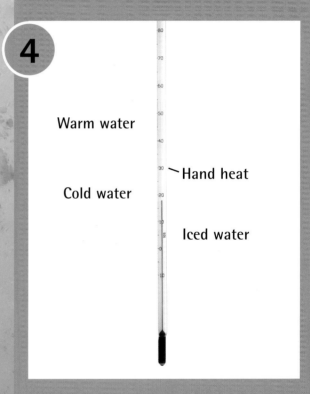

Warm water

Cold water

Hand heat

Iced water

What do you think?

You can find out how cold something is by feeling it, or you can measure its temperature with a thermometer. Which is the most accurate?

Heat conductors

Stone, glass and metals are good conductors of heat. Glass is made by heating sand. The most common metals are iron and steel. Steel is a mixture of iron and other materials.

Taking in heat

A good conductor quickly takes in heat and passes it on. If you touch something made of stone on a hot day, the stone feels hot. This is because the heat from the stone quickly moves into your fingers. However, on a cold day the stone takes heat away from your fingers. This makes the stone feel cold.

In hot, sunny countries, a stone can become so hot you can fry an egg on it!

Glass

When someone has a hot shower, the bathroom mirror becomes misty. This is because some of the hot water has turned into the **gas, water vapou**r. When the water vapour touches the glass, the glass takes heat from it. The vapour cools and **condenses**. It changes into tiny water droplets.

Mirrors are made of glass, a good conductor of heat. This bathroom mirror is misty with water droplets.

The heat race

You will need:

A metal teaspoon, a small plastic spoon, a wooden spoon or lollipop stick, margarine or butter, 3 dried peas, a mug, a saucepan of water, an oven thermometer, and a clock or watch.

This experiment tests different materials to see which is the best conductor. To make the test fair, use spoons that are about the same size. Which material do you think will be the best conductor? Ask an adult to help you heat and pour the water.

Put a small lump of butter on the top of each spoon. Perch a dried pea in each lump. Put the spoons in the mug.

1

Heat up 250 ml of water in the pan until it reaches at least 80° Celsius (use the thermometer to check).

2

Ask the adult to half fill the mug with the water. After a while the spoons will conduct the heat to the butter.

Time how long it takes before the first pea falls off a spoon. Which material is the spoon made of? That material is the best conductor!

3

4

WARNING:
This investigation uses hot water – make sure you have an adult to help you.

Hot drinks and straws

Never suck hot drinks through a straw. To see why, pour some hot water into a mug and put a straw in it. Feel the top of the straw with your fingers. It feels cool, but the hot liquid would burn your mouth.

Using heat conductors

Metal is the best heat conductor. Iron and steel are used for cooking pots, irons, radiators and many other things that conduct heat. A hot iron smoothes out the creases in crumpled clothes. The iron's metal plate conducts the heat onto the clothes.

Be careful not to touch a hot iron. It will burn you.

Cooking

Pots and pans are made of metal because they quickly conduct heat from the cooker to the food. Some pans are made of **copper**, because copper is a better conductor than iron or steel. However, copper is more expensive than steel. Metal is a good material to use in cooking because it does not catch fire, and it melts only at very high temperatures. **Barbeques** have a metal grid to hold the food over the hot **charcoal**.

Radiators

Central heating radiators are usually made of iron or steel. They become warm when hot water is pumped through them. The metal conducts the heat from the water to warm the air around the radiator.

Turn on a cold central heating radiator. Track the heat as it moves through the radiator. Which way is the water flowing?

Holding heat in

Many kinds of material are good insulators. An insulator takes in heat slowly and stays warm. It does not pass the heat on quickly. For example, the underside of many **table mats** are covered with **cork**, because cork is a good insulator. The cork protects the table from hot dishes.

These mats are made of wood and cork. Both of these materials are good insulators.

Fabrics

Many fabrics are good insulators. Wool and cotton are natural fabrics. Wool comes from sheep and other animals. Cotton is made from the fluffy fibres of cotton plants. Many **synthetic materials** are made from **oil**. Many sleeping bags and winter coats are padded with synthetic materials that are good insulators.

A padded coat and trousers will keep you warm on a cold day. They hold in the warmth of your body.

Which of these hats is likely to keep your head the warmest? How would you test your theory?

Air

Air is one of the best insulators. Materials that are good insulators often contain air. For example, cork and wool contain little pockets of air. Many synthetic materials, such as polystyrene, contain air too. Some take-away cups are made of polystyrene because the polystyrene will keep the hot drink hot for longer than a paper cup. In the straw test on page 11, the drinking straw does not conduct heat and the air in the empty straw acts as an insulator.

Using air to insulate

Many good insulators contain air. Birds fluff out their feathers when they are cold. The feathers trap air, which keeps in the heat of their bodies. Duvets use air in the same way. Some duvets are actually stuffed with feathers, while other duvets are stuffed with synthetic material.

What happens when you shake a duvet? Does it get thicker or thinner? Why? Will this make it a better insulator or not?

This bird is puffing out its feathers to keep itself warm.

Double-glazed windows

Buildings can lose a lot of heat through their glass windows. To stop this happening many windows are **double-glazed**. This means that they have two panes of glass, with either a layer of air or a gas called **argon** trapped between them. Triple-glazing uses three panes of glass with gas trapped between them. Very little heat escapes through triple-glazing!

The windows of this older house are being changed to double-glazed windows.

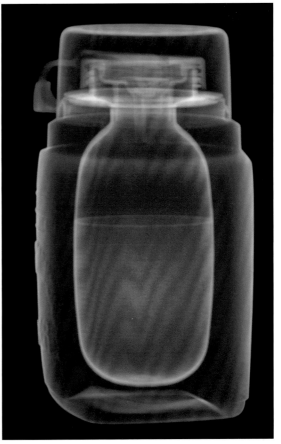

Vacuum flask

A **vacuum** flask can keep liquids hot or cold for several hours. The flask is made of two layers of glass, metal or plastic, with nothing between them – not even air! The air is taken out and the flask sealed, leaving a vacuum. A vacuum is a good insulator because there is nothing to pass the heat on.

This coloured X-ray shows how a vacuum flask is one container inside another.

Insulating an animal's den

You will need:

3 identical take-away cups with lids; two identical boxes that are a bit bigger than the cups; dried leaves; compost; hot water; a thermometer; a clock; paper and a pencil; newspaper.

Many animals make a **den** in which to spend the cold months of winter. This experiment tests whether dried leaves or compost make the best insulator for an animal's den. Which do you think it will be?

Ask an adult to fill each cup with hot water and put the lid on. Put one cup of hot water in each box. Leave one cup as it is.

Fill the space between one of the cups and the box with dried leaves. Fill the space in the other box with compost.

Measure the temperature of the liquid in each cup by carefully pushing the thermometer through the hole in the lids. Record the temperatures in a table.

Measure the temperatures again every 5 minutes up to 20 minutes. Which cup stayed warmest? Was your guess right? How did they compare with the uninsulated cup?

3

4

A different material

Try the experiment again using torn up, loosely crumpled newspaper as an insulator. How does it compare with the leaves and compost?

Insulating homes

About a third of the heat in most homes is wasted. Double-glazing cuts down heat lost through windows, but heat also escapes through the roof and walls. Insulation keeps homes warm in winter and cool in summer.

Insulating roofs

In the past some roofs were covered with **thatch** made of straw or reeds (some still are today). The thatch helped to insulate the roof. Today, insulation is placed inside a roof, in the **loft**. A thick layer of insulating material is laid on the floor of the loft. It stops warm air leaking out through the ceiling.

The floor of a loft is covered with insulating material.

This cottage has a thatched roof.

Fill a plastic bag with hay. Place a small plastic box, filled with hot water and with the lid on, inside the hay. Put another one on the table next to it. Guess how long each one will take to cool down and then time them both.

Insulating walls

Most houses built in the last 80 years have two outside walls with a gap between them. These are called **cavity walls**. Air in the gap stops heat being conducted though the wall. When the gap is filled with foam or another insulating material, it works even better.

This new house is being built with a cavity wall. The bricks have air spaces in them, too.

Keeping things cold

Insulators are used to keep things cold as well as to keep things hot. The ground is a good insulator. In the past people dug deep holes in the ground and filled them with ice in winter. The ice slowly melted, but it kept food fresh until summer. Today we use fridges, freezers and **cold bags** to keep food cold.

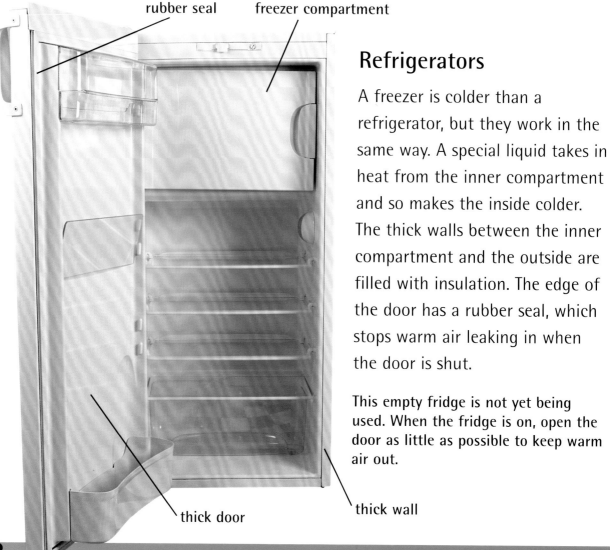

rubber seal   freezer compartment

thick door

thick wall

Refrigerators

A freezer is colder than a refrigerator, but they work in the same way. A special liquid takes in heat from the inner compartment and so makes the inside colder. The thick walls between the inner compartment and the outside are filled with insulation. The edge of the door has a rubber seal, which stops warm air leaking in when the door is shut.

This empty fridge is not yet being used. When the fridge is on, open the door as little as possible to keep warm air out.

Cold bags

Cold bags can keep food and drinks cold for up to several hours. Cold bags use different materials, such as foam, sheep's wool and shiny foil, to insulate the inside.

Cold bags are handy for picnics.

Make your own cold bag. Put a chilled bottle of water in a plastic bag and wrap it in bubble wrap. Put the wrapped bottle into a bigger plastic bag. How long does the drink stay cool?

Staying cool

This experiment compares three materials to see which is the best insulator. To make sure the experiment is a fair test, cut just enough of each material to cover an ice cube. Use a spare ice cube to test the size.

You will need:

Ice cubes, bubble wrap, aluminium foil, newspaper, sticky tape, an oven tray, scissors, a clock or watch, light-bulb box, kitchen towel.

Wrap an ice cube in the bubble wrap. Leave a gap at the bottom of the cube. Wrap sticky tape around the sides to hold it in place. Wrap another cube in aluminium foil.

Cut four pieces of newspaper and put them one on top of the other. Wrap a third ice cube in them.

Put all three ice cubes on an oven tray, with the gap in the wrapping face down.

3

Which cube begins to melt first? Which one melts last? Check by lifting each ice cube to see if any water has collected beneath it.

4

Double insulation

Wrap an ice cube in the material that was the best insulator. Fill an empty light-bulb box with crumpled kitchen towel. Place the ice cube in the middle of the box. How long does the ice take to melt completely?

Building materials

Often buildings are made of materials that are found **locally**. For example, homes in the mountains are often made of wood, if they are near forests, or of stone. Bricks are one of the cheapest materials. They are made from clay, which is a kind of mud, and baked in a hot oven.

This house in the mountains of Switzerland is built of thick stone and wood.

The best insulators

Wood and mud are very good insulators. In hot countries it is often very hot during the day and cold at night. Here, many **traditional** homes are made of mud. In some countries mud is made into bricks without baking them. This is called **adobe**. During the day the mud takes in heat and keeps the house cool. At night it slowly gives up its heat, making the house warm.

This building is made of adobe, or mud.

Concrete

All over the world, offices and tall blocks of flats are made of concrete and glass. This is because concrete is easy to work with and it can be made into all kinds of shapes. However, concrete is not a good insulator. Offices which have a lot of glass have to use double-glazing to stop the inside getting too hot or too cold.

Which building is better insulated – the wooden house below or the concrete block of flats above?

Super insulators

Astronauts, **mountaineers** and scuba divers go to places that are extremely hot or cold. They wear clothes and special suits that are very good insulators.

Spacesuits

As a spacecraft orbits the Earth, it becomes burning hot in the sunshine and then freezing cold in the dark. When astronauts work outside the spacecraft or space station, they have to wear spacesuits. The suits keep out the heat of the Sun and keep in the heat of the astronaut's body.

Scuba divers wear wet suits to insulate them from the cold water. A wet suit allows a small amount of water to pass through it and form an insulating layer.

A spacesuit provides everything an astronaut needs to stay alive outside the spacecraft. It is made from several layers of synthetic material.

Blizzard bags

Blizzard bags are particularly good at keeping in warmth. They are used by mountaineers, the army and rescue teams. The bag is made of stretchy synthetic material that clings to the body. It has triangular channels that trap air and so it works a bit like bubble wrap. The material is very light and the blizzard bag can be squashed up small when it is not being used.

This blizzard bag is twice as warm as most sleeping bags.

Glossary

adobe Bricks made of mud and dried in the sun.

argon An invisible gas that is found in the air and which is used in some double-glazing.

barbeque An open-air fire of burning charcoal used for grilling meat.

cavity wall An outside wall of a building that consists of two brick walls with a gap between them.

charcoal Fuel made of partly burned wood.

cold bag Bag for keeping food cold.

condense Change from a gas into a liquid.

conductor Something that passes on heat.

copper A reddish brown metal that conducts heat well.

cork The outer layer of the bark of a cork oak; cork is light in weight and is a good insulator.

den Sheltered place used by a wild animal. The animal often insulates its den with leaves, feathers or other natural materials.

double-glazed With two layers of glass.

gas Form of matter that is neither solid nor liquid.

insulator Something that holds in heat.

locally From the same place.

loft A space or room underneath the roof of a house, which is often used for storage.

mountaineer Person who climbs mountains.

oil Liquid that is found in the ground and is used as fuel and to make synthetic materials.

synthetic material Material that has been manufactured; synthetic materials include plastic, concrete and polystyrene.

table mat Flat piece of insulating material used to protect tables from hot plates and dishes.

temperature A measure of how hot something is.

thatch Roofing material made of bundles of reeds or straw tied together.

thermometer An instrument for measuring temperature.

traditional Following methods or customs that have been handed down from one generation to another.

vacuum Empty space from which nearly all the air and other gases have been removed.

water vapour Water in the form of gas.

Some answers

Page 6/7: If the water feels warm to your hand, it is likely that its temperature is higher than that of your hand. The iced water is probably the coldest measurement. Using a thermometer gives a more accurate measurement of heat than feeling it with your hand.

Page 11: The metal spoon should win the heat race. The top of the straw feels cool because the straw is not a good conductor. It does not tell you how hot the liquid is.

Page 13: Heat moves from the end of the radiator with the valve to the other end. A valve is a kind of tap that allows you to turn the radiator off.

Page 15: The woollen hat is the warmest of these hats. Test your own selection of hats, by seeing which one keeps a hard-boiled egg warm for longest. Ask an adult to hard boil several eggs – one for each hat. Cover each egg with a hat. Which one stays warm the longest?

Page 16: When you shake a duvet it becomes thicker, because more air is trapped by the material inside it. The extra air will make the duvet a better insulator.

Page 19: Both of the cups surrounded by insulating material should have stayed warm longer than the cup on its own. It is likely that the cup surrounded by leaves stayed the warmest. It is likely that the crumpled newspaper is a better insulator than the leaves or the compost.

Page 21: How long the water takes to cool down depends on how big the box is. But the box buried in the hay will stay warmer longer than the box on its own.

Page 23: How long the bottle stays cool depends on how many layers of bubble wrap you have used. With several layers of bubble wrap, the bottle is likely to stay cool for several hours.

Page 25: The cube wrapped in newspaper will begin to melt first. The cube wrapped in bubble wrap will melt last. With double insulation, the cube will last much longer before it begins to melt. In fact, you might get bored waiting for it to happen!

Page 27: The wooden building is probably better insulated, particularly if it has double cavity walls and double-glazed windows.

Index

Further information

www.primaryresources.co.uk/science/
science3a.htm
Website for teachers with links to resources on many aspects of materials, including thermal conductors and insulators.

www.sciencetech.technomuses.ca/english/
schoolzone/materials.cfm
A site about materials attached to the Canadian Science and Technology Museum in Ottawa.

www.sciencekids.co.nz/gamesactivities/
keepingwarm.html
Includes an interactive experiment that allows you to compare how well different materials insulate a beaker. This New Zealand site also includes experiments and facts as well as games and activities.

http://home.howstuffworks.com/thermos2.htm
Explains how a thermos flask works.

http://science.nasa.gov/headlines/y2001/
ast21mar_1.htm
A Nasa website that looks at how space stations and homes on Earth are insulated.

www.bbc.co.uk/schools/ks2bitesize/science/
materials.shtml
Activities and quiz about materials for children aged 7 to 11.